Rookie reader

Sand

By Pam Miller

Illustrated by Rick Stromoski

Children's Press®
A Division of Grolier Publishing
New York • London • Hong Kong • Sydney
Danbury, Connecticut

To my family, my friends, and my writers' group.
Thanks for your support and enthusiasm all along the way.
—P. M.

To Molly
—R. S.

Reading Consultants
Linda Cornwell
Coordinator of School Quality and Professional Improvement
(Indiana State Teachers Association)

Katharine A. Kane
Education Consultant
(Retired, San Diego County Office of Education
and San Diego State University)

Visit Children's Press® on the Internet at:
http://publishing.grolier.com

Library of Congress Cataloging-in-Publication Data
Miller, Pamela Ann.
    Sand / by Pam Miller ; illustrated by Rick Stromoski.
       p. cm. — (Rookie reader)
    Summary: Describes the many uses of sand, what it looks like, where it is found, and how it is formed.
    ISBN 0-516-22013-6 (lib. bdg.)   0-516-27079-6 (pbk.)
    1. Sand—Juvenile literature. [1. Sand.] I. Stromoski, Rick, ill. II. Title. III. Series.
TN939.M557 2000
553.6'22—dc21   99-054170

GROLIER
PUBLISHING
   3 4 5 6 7 8 9 10 R 09 08 07 06 05 04 03 02

Sand in my bucket.

3

Sand on the beach.

Sand in the desert,
far from our reach.

Piles of sand.

Miles of sand,

stretch from here

to there.

Sand used in building
roads everywhere.

Bags of sand

14

hold back a flood.

They keep out water.
They keep out mud.

White sand.
Black sand.

Pink sand or gold.

Wet sand.

Dry sand.

Hot sand

or cold.

The wind blows.

The waves roar.

The rocks break
and turn to sand
on the shore.

These tiny, tiny rocks
make a hill in your hand.

These tiny, tiny rocks
are what we call sand!

Word List (61 words)

a	flood	roads
and	from	roar
are	gold	rocks
back	hand	sand
bags	here	shore
beach	hill	stretch
black	hold	the
blows	hot	there
break	in	these
bucket	keep	they
building	make	tiny
call	miles	to
cold	mud	turn
desert	my	used
dry	of	water
everywhere	on	waves
far	or	we
	our	wet
	out	what
	piles	white
	pink	wind
	reach	your

About the Author

Pam Miller lives in Gaithersburg, Maryland. She and her husband have a son and a daughter, Chris and Elizabeth. Pam has taught preschool for many years and she spends every summer at the beach with her family, playing in the sand.

About the Illustrator

Rick Stromoski is an award-winning humorous illustrator whose work has appeared in magazines, newspapers, children's books, advertising, and network television. He lives in Suffield, Connecticut, with his wife, Danna, and five-year-old daughter, Molly.